Defoe Abbott Marx Hardy Machiavelli Montaigne Chesterton Cooper Emerson Joyce Austen Hugo Eliot Grimm
Melville Carroll Christie Haggard Molière
Stoker Wilde Maupassant Byron Schiller
Garnett Einstein Fitzgerald Engels Smith Kafka Hall Willis
Goethe Hawthorne
Cotton Dostoyevsky
Baum Henry Kipling Doyle
Leslie Dumas Nietzsche
Flaubert Turgenev Balzac
Stockton Vatsyayana Crane
Burroughs Verne
Curtis Tocqueville Vinci
Homer Widger Tolstoy Gogol Busch
Darwin Thoreau Whitman
Potter Freud Zola Twain Plato Scott Harte
Kant Jowett Lawrence Dickens Hesse
Stevenson Burton
Andersen
London Descartes Voltaire Cervantes
Poe Aristotle Wells Cooke
Hale James Hastings
Bunner Shakespeare Irving
Richter Chambers Alcott
Doré Dante Chekhov da Shaw Wodehouse Benedict
Swift Pushkin
Newton

 tredition®

tredition was established in 2006 by Sandra Latusseck and Soenke Schulz. Based in Hamburg, Germany, tredition offers publishing solutions to authors and publishing houses, combined with world-wide distribution of printed and digital book content. tredition is uniquely positioned to enable authors and publishing houses to create books on their own terms and without conventional manu-facturing risks.

For more information please visit: www.tredition.com

TREDITION CLASSICS

This book is part of the TREDITION CLASSICS series. The creators of this series are united by passion for literature and driven by the intention of making all public domain books available in printed format again - worldwide. Most TREDITION CLASSICS titles have been out of print and off the bookstore shelves for decades. At tredition we believe that a great book never goes out of style and that its value is eternal. Several mostly non-profit literature projects provide content to tredition. To support their good work, tredition donates a portion of the proceeds from each sold copy. As a reader of a TREDITION CLASSICS book, you support our mission to save many of the amazing works of world literature from oblivion. See all available books at www.tredition.com.

Project Gutenberg

The content for this book has been graciously provided by Project Gutenberg. Project Gutenberg is a non-profit organization founded by Michael Hart in 1971 at the University of Illinois. The mission of Project Gutenberg is simple: To encourage the creation and distribu-tion of eBooks. Project Gutenberg is the first and largest collection of public domain eBooks.

Vigée Le Brun

Haldane MacFall

Imprint

This book is part of TREDITION CLASSICS

Author: Haldane MacFall
Cover design: Buchgut, Berlin – Germany

Publisher: tredition GmbH, Hamburg - Germany
ISBN: 978-3-8472-1237-9

www.tredition.com
www.tredition.de

Vigée Le Brun

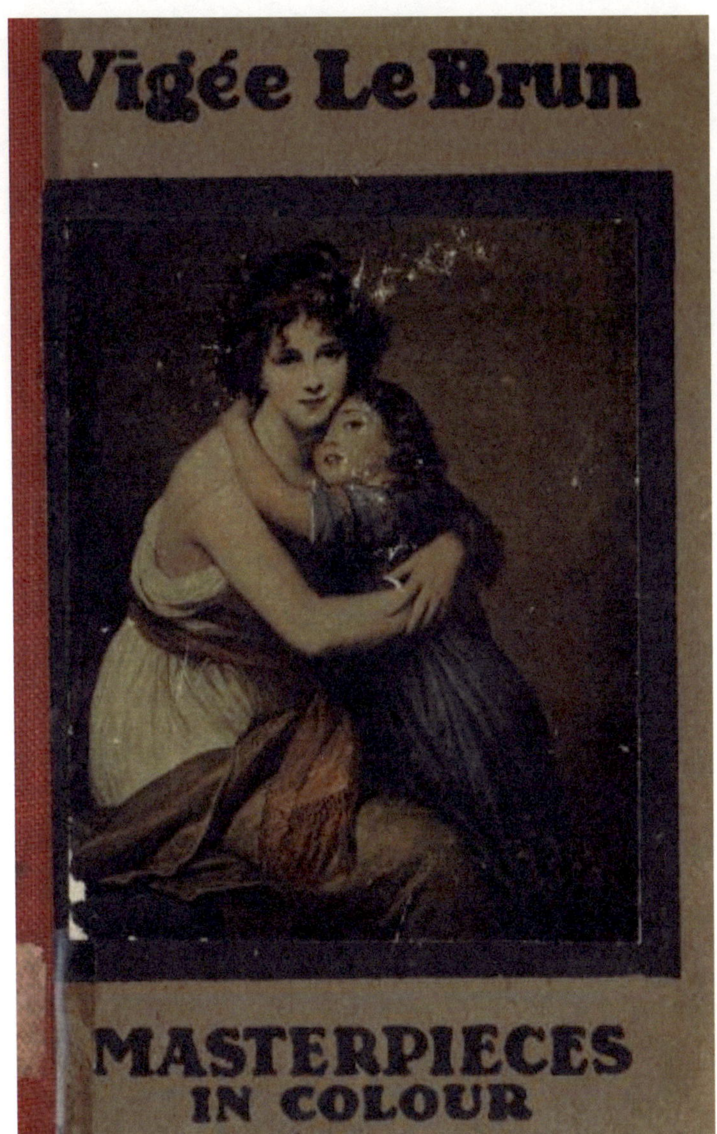

MASTERPIECES
IN COLOUR

MASTERPIECES
IN COLOUR
EDITED BY —
T. LEMAN HARE

VIGÉE LE BRUN
1755-1842

PLATE I. — MARIE ANTOINETTE. Frontispiece

(At Versailles)

The first portrait that Vigée Le Brun painted, in her twenty-fourth year (1779) of Marie Antoinette. Here is no hint of the tragedy that was to overwhelm the handsome young daughter of Austria; all was as yet but gaiety and roses and sunshine and pleasant airs, and the glamour that hovers about a throne. But there are signs of the imperious temper of her house, combined with the levity and frivolity of manners which were so early to make her unpopular.

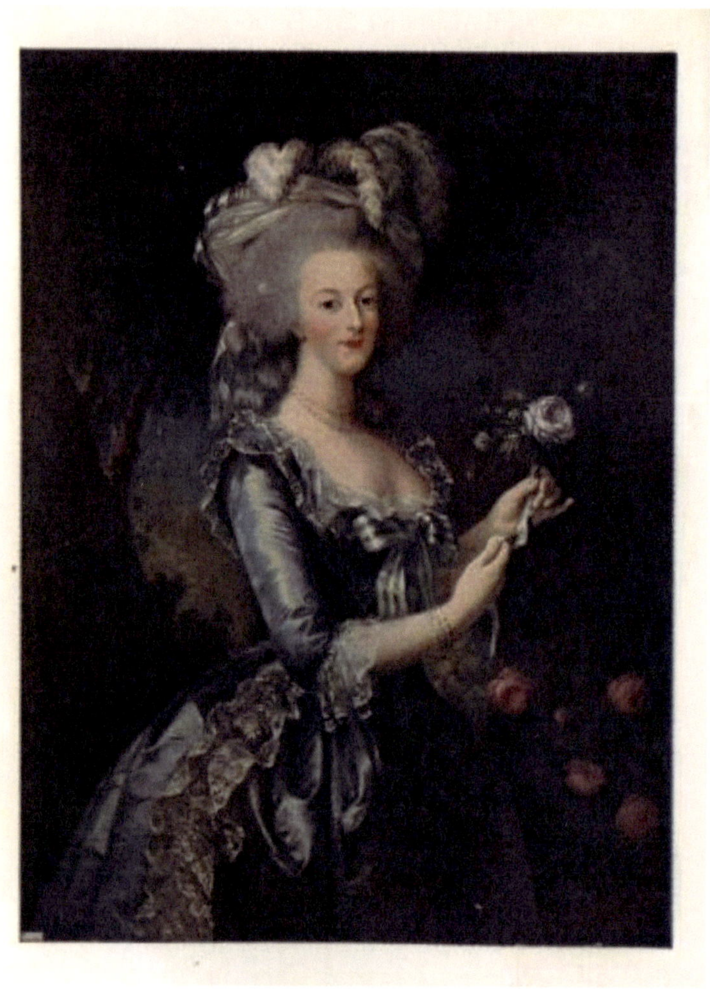

Vigée Le Brun

BY HALDANE MACFALL

ILLUSTRATED WITH EIGHT
REPRODUCTIONS IN COLOUR

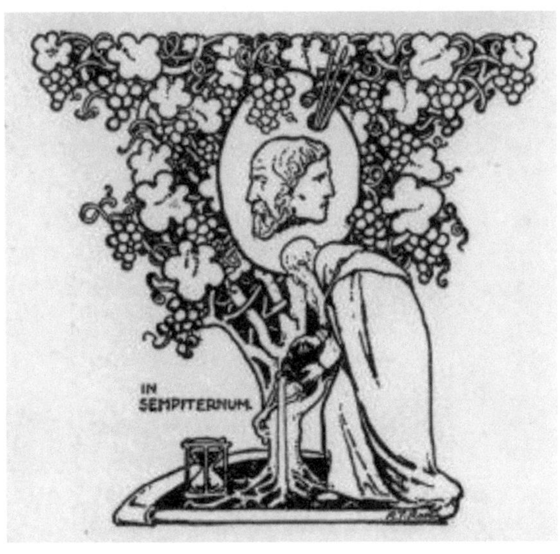

LONDON: T. C. & E. C. JACK
NEW YORK: FREDERICK A. STOKES CO.
1907

CONTENTS

LIST OF ILLUSTRATIONS

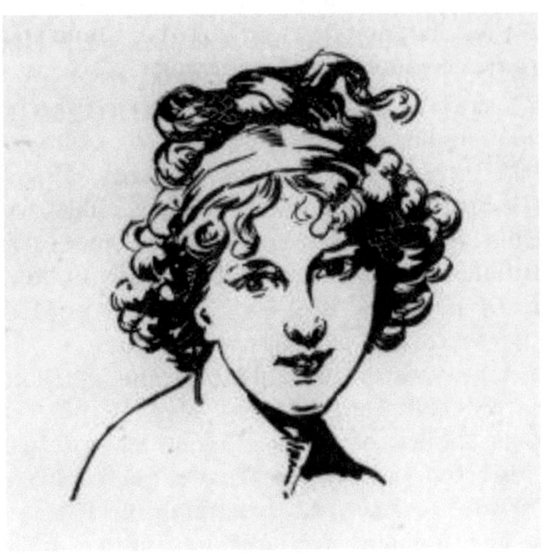

I

THE BEGINNINGS

In Paris, in the Rue Coquillière, Louis the Fifteenth being King of France—or rather the Pompadour holding sway thereover—there lived a witty, amiable fellow who plied the art of painting portraits in oils and pastels after the mediocre fashion that is called "pleasing." This Louis Vigée and his wife, Jeanne Maissin, moved in the genial enthusiastic circle of the lesser artists, passing through their sober day without undue excitement; for fame and wealth and the prizes of life were not for them. Boucher was lord of art; and La Tour and Greuze and Chardin were at the height of their genius; but honest Louis Vigée could but plod on at his pleasing portraits, and sigh that the gods had not borne to him the immortal flame.

Yet he was to come near to the glory of it—nearer than he thought. 'Twas a pity that he was robbed of the splendour of basking in the reflected radiance, and by a fish's bone.

It was to have its beginning in that year after the indolent but obstinate king, having fallen foul of his Parliaments in his game of facing-both-ways in the bitter strife 'twixt Church and people, patched up a peace with the Parliament men.

PLATE II. — MADAME VIGÉE LE BRUN AND CHILD

(In the Louvre)

In Vigée Le Brun's portrait of herself and her child we see in full career the Greek ideals that were come upon France — a France weary of light trifling with life, and of mere butterfly flitting from flower to flower.

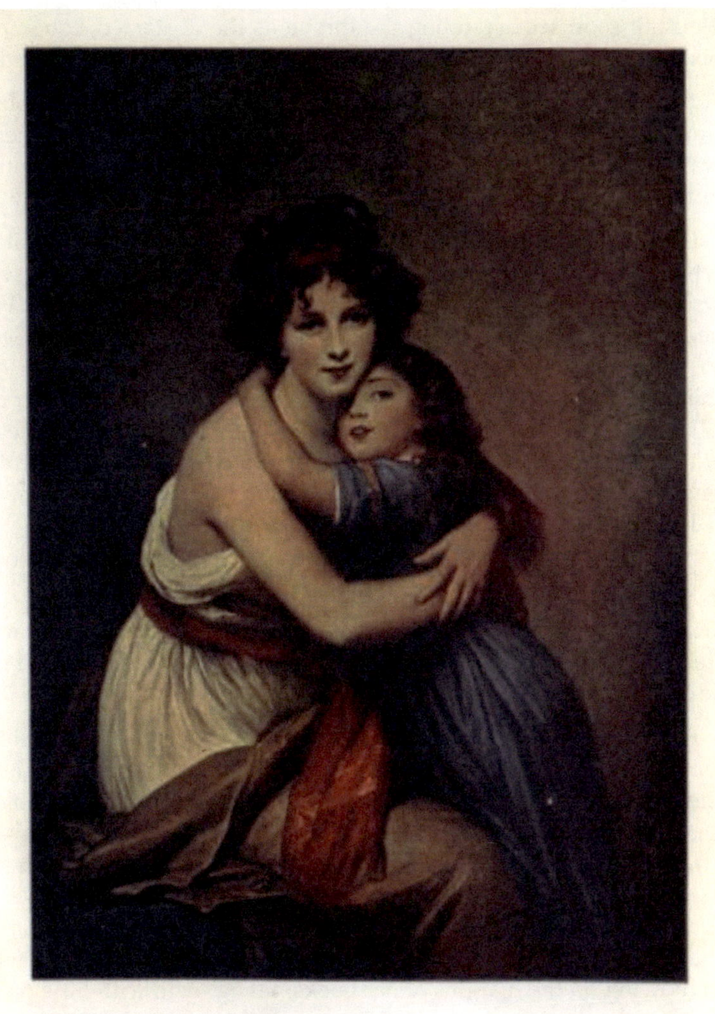

Our worthy mediocre Vigée could remember the banished Parliament re-entering Paris in triumph on that fourth day of September in 1754 amidst the exultant shouts of the people; the clergy looking on with a scowl the while. On that same day was born to the Dauphin a son—the little fellow called the Duke de Berry—whom we shall soon see ascending the throne as the ill-starred Louis the Sixteenth, for the Dauphin was to be taken before the old king died.

Honest waggish Vigée, painting industriously at his pleasing portraits, would recall it well; since, early in the following year, there was that to happen under his own modest roof which was to bring fame to his name, though he should not live to bask in its full glow.

On the 10th of April 1755 there was born to him a little girl-child, whom they christened Elizabeth Louise Vigée, or as she herself wrote it across the title-page of her *Souvenirs*, Louise Elizabeth Vigée. Into her little fingers Destiny set the skill that had been denied to her father; the flame was given to her. And by the whimsy of things, there was also born in far-away Vienna, in this same year of 1755, in the palace of the Emperors of Austria, a little princess whom they christened Marie Antoinette; who was to marry the little seven-month old princeling that lay sucking his thumb in the Royal palace near by, and thereby to become future Queen of France.

Like François Boucher, the great painter to the king, Elizabeth Vigée came to the pretty business with the advantage of being an artist's child; like him, she received her first lessons at an early age from her father; and, like him, she moved from earliest childhood in an atmosphere of art and artists.

From her father she inherited a talent and taste for art, an amiable temper, a gift of wit; from her mother, a very handsome woman, she was dowered with a beauty for which she was as remarkable, and to which her many portraits of herself bear abundant witness. From very childhood she began to display the proofs of her inheritance—that happy disposition and that charm of manner that were to make her one of the most winsome personalities of her time. At the convent to which her parents sent her in her tenth year she fell to drawing on the margins of her books, filling them with little portrait-heads—an incessant habit that set her teachers grumbling at her lack of respect towards grammar and history. But to her delighted father the grumbles were matter for laughter; in him she found an ally who was hugely proud to discover in his girl an inheritor of his gifts. It is told of the fond father that the girl having taken to him one day a drawing, Vigée cried out exultantly: "You will be a painter, my girl, or there never was one!"

Brought up, as the child was, in the world of artists, with the aims and ambitions and enthusiasms of artists for her very breath, she could not fail to find in such a world, besides the encouragement which was prodigally bestowed upon so young and promising a talent, the teaching needful to develop her powers. Amongst the artists who were on friendly terms with the girl's father, and of whom Doyen was the most intimate, was Davesne, a member and deputy professor of the Academy of St. Luke — he who afterwards claimed to have taught the little Elizabeth the elements of painting. Davesne's lessons were at best but few, and seem to have been limited to showing the eager child how to set a palette. The girl was in fact picking up the crumbs that fell from many tables; at any rate she showed astoundingly precocious industry and gifts, and was soon making quite a stir amongst the painter-folk, and becoming a source of pride to her father.

Vigée, however, was only destined to guide and encourage the child towards the path; he died on the 9th of May 1768 from swallowing a fish bone. Little Elizabeth was but thirteen years old when this first great grief fell upon her.

That was a strange world in which the child stood bewildered at the baffling cruelty of human destiny — this eighteenth-century France. The Pompadour had died in the child's ninth year; her dogged and persistent enemy, the Dauphin, the year after her; the neglected queen now followed the Pompadour to the grave in the June of this same year that left little Elizabeth fatherless.

Under the scandals of the Court, and the tyranny and corruption of the nobility and clergy, the French people were no longer concealing their distress under courtly phrases, nor groaning in secret. The ideas of the new philosophers were penetrating and colouring public opinion. They were beginning to talk of the great antique days of Greece, of heroes, and of virtue, and of living and dying like Romans. Fickle fashion was turning her back upon the art of old Boucher, and upon Dresden shepherds and shepherdesses and pleasant landscapes and bosky groves, and was taking up her abode with heroes and amongst picturesque ruins. The Parliament men were demanding rights, were indeed going to prison and into banishment for those rights; nay, was not Choiseul the great minister of

France; and Choiseul's power was deep planted in the rights of the people and founded on Parliaments. All France was watching for the dawn of liberty.

II

THE WONDERFUL CHILD

The thirteen-year-old child suffered a grief so poignant at the loss of her father, to whom she had been passionately attached, that it threatened to have the gravest consequences on her future; had it not been for her father's old friend Doyen, who, transferring to the girl the deep affection he had had for the dead man, urged the child to take up her brushes again—for she was already painting from Nature.

It was now that she entered the studio of Gabriel Briard, an historical painter and member of the Royal Academy; a mediocre artist (though superior to Davesne, who claimed to have been her teacher), but he was a fine draughtsman.

To Briard's studio she went with a little friend, a year older than herself, Mademoiselle Bocquet, who was to become like herself a member of the Academy of Saint Luke; a girl of a certain talent who, however, abandoned painting on her early marriage.

The two girls tripped it to Briard's studio like a couple of school-children, demurely escorted by a servant, who carried their dinner in a basket; and, as they went to their daily task, be sure the quick intelligent girl heard more than a little scandal of the Court—indeed all Paris more than whispered of it—scandal big with meaning for France, and for little Elizabeth not least of all.

The tears of the king's grief over the dead body of his queen were scarce dried when Louis the Fifteenth still further degraded the dignity of the throne of France—still more dangerously brought royalty into contempt by publicly acknowledging as his new mistress a young woman from the gutters, the beautiful, laughing, reckless spendthrift Du Barry, to whom one of the king's first gifts was

Louveciennes, where Elizabeth was afterwards to meet her. Before the year was out Choiseul fell; and for the remaining four years that were left to the king France was governed by the milliner Du Barry and her precious trio, D'Aiguillon, Terray, and Maupeou; and rushed towards the abyss.

However, these things troubled our precocious Elizabeth but little as yet. The girl grew rapidly in craftsmanship and in personal beauty. Indeed, she developed towards womanhood as early and as swiftly as in skill of artistry, being remarkable for her prettiness, her freshness and delicacy of colouring, and her elegance of figure — early displaying the airy wit that, with these abundant gifts of her fairy godmother, were so valuable an aid to the reputation which she was achieving by her artistry at a time when most children are in the schoolroom.

Her advance was so astounding that every one was talking about the girl; and the moment soon arrived when her master saw the pupil passing him in skill of hand and reputation as a painter; gazing dumbfounded at the stream of the greatest celebrities and personages of the day flocking to the studio of a girl of but fifteen years of age.

How strange a thing the weaving of the web of Destiny! In this very same year there came out of Austria a fifteen-year-old princess of its Royal House, leaving the home of her forefathers in tears, and amidst the tears of a people that had grown to love the winsome child; for, Marie Antoinette was setting forth on her life's adventure as future Queen of France, a tragic wayfaring for a butterfly!

Elizabeth Vigée's extraordinary rise into notice brought her the friendship and counsel of Joseph Vernet, who gave her most precious advice which was a beacon to her career all her years: "My child," said he, "do not follow any system of schools. Consult only the works of the great Italian and Flemish masters. But, above all things, make as many studies as you can from Nature. Nature is the supreme master. If you study Nature with care it will prevent you from picking up any mannerisms."

PLATE III. — MADAME VIGÉE LE BRUN AND CHILD

(In the Louvre)

Vigée Le Brun painted another portrait of herself and her little girl-child; and she painted both, fortunately for her fame, when her skill was at its increase. They stand out, with all their limitations, pure and exquisite as the Madonna and Child of Italy's finest achievement; for they were painted by a woman of genius with the passionate love of a child that is the wondrous heritage of woman — none the less religious in that it apes no show of religion.

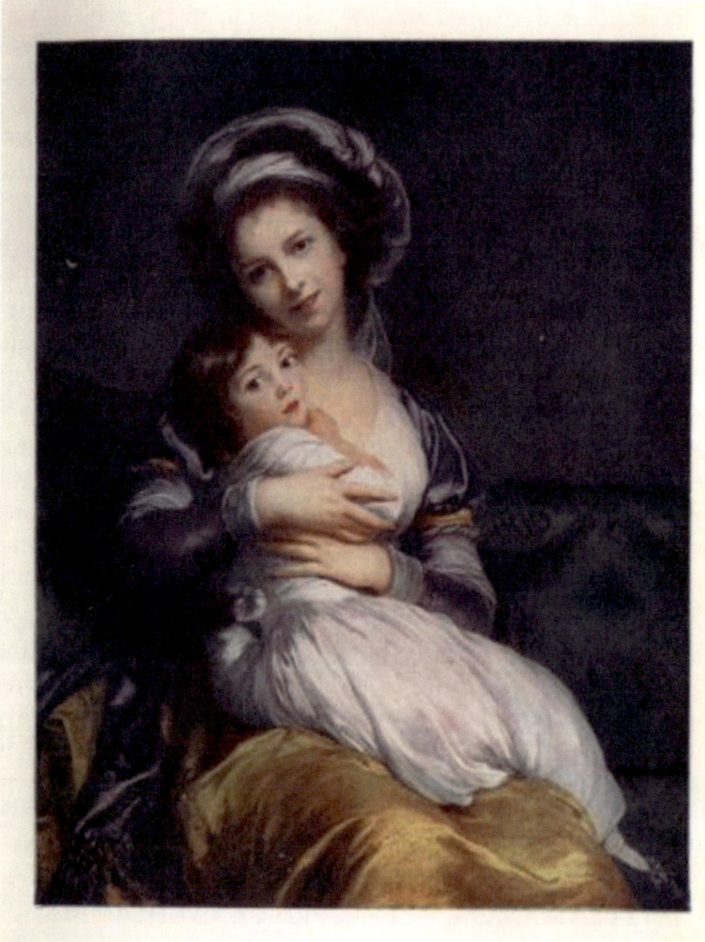

Doyen and Greuze also helped her with suggestions; but she was from the beginning her own teacher. Davesne and Briard only flattered themselves by claiming her tutoring. The girl showed in no way any slightest sign of their influence. Ardent and enthusiastic in her pursuit of art, she haunted the galleries and private collections, but above all she went to Nature. Naturalness is by consequence a marked attribute of one who painted in this artificial age—in portraiture she largely escaped the conventional style, both its limitations and, be it also confessed, something of that great beauty of style and that superb decorative splendour that mark the handsome achievement of Nattier and Drouais and their fellows. Nor must it be forgotten that the realism claimed by the later years, and the naturalism claimed for this girl's art, were already to be seen in full career in the master-work of La Tour in portraiture, and in the still-life of Chardin. This girl's genius never reached to the force of La Tour, nor the superb handling or colour-sense or vigour of Chardin, but she painted with rare skill the eminent women of her day and, with near as remarkable a skill, more than one man; her loss would have left a serious gap in the statement of the French genius of the end of the seventeen hundreds.

It has been a custom too long indulged in by literary critics to praise her at the expense of Boucher's "conventionality"; but she never painted a portrait that surpassed the Wallace "Pompadour" or the "Infant Orleans," to say nothing of other rare portraits from Boucher's easel. To set her up in rivalry against one of the greatest decorative artists of the years is but to give her an ugly fall. The astounding part is not that she painted better than she did, but that she achieved what she did.

But free from convention? No. She was a woman, and a painter of women—a painter of women from the woman's point of view that desires the world only to think of woman in her pose as woman, reticent, careful to screen the impulsive, most of all the vexatious, the violent, and the irregular moods of femininity's temperament from the eyes of the passer-by; always eager to show woman dressed for the part, and well dressed. She was incapable of stating the deeps of character; and had she had the power, she would have looked upon it as something of an indecency—or worse, an indelicacy. She would, in fact, have preferred to deny the deeps. She sets her sitter ever in the drawing-room of fashion, draws a heavy curtain with a rattle between the drawing-room and the inner boudoir (the "sulking room"), slams the door on the bedroom, or any hint that there is a bedroom, before she cries "come in," to admit us to her studio; she prefers to show the woman in her properties as the creature of fashion, not in the intimacy of her inner living and full significance.

This is as much and as absolutely convention as any tricking out of ladies as Dresden shepherdesses, and the more subtle in that it is the less obvious; as much convention as any painting of large eyes or rose-bud mouths. It is as misleading as convention. But it is the basis of a woman's life; and, in that, it is true.

Boucher has been blamed for being conventional; is often sneered at as the arch-make-believe. But when he painted women he painted them as men really see them with their masks off, and with all their allure of femininity. This sneer of convention is a two-edged sword.

In the year that they found Boucher dead, seated at his easel before an unfinished canvas of Venus, this girl of fifteen discovered herself celebrated; saw her studio invaded by the flower of the world of fashion; the women of the nobility at the French Court visiting her; the exclusive doors of the Faubourg St. Germain thrown open to her; princesses, duchesses, countesses, celebrities of the day and strangers of distinction her friends. She was in close touch with the leading artists of her day—Le Moyne, blunt Quentin de La Tour, and the rest.

The girl, in spite of her astounding industry, was soon wholly unable to carry out the orders for portraits which rained in upon her; her charm of manner and her increasing beauty added to the pressure of the siege of her admirers.

A little while before her fifteenth birthday her mother married again a young jeweller, of the name of Le Sèvre, a miserly fellow, who, under the pretext of taking them into the country, hired a little house at Chaillot, where they went with the girl for their Sundays; the thrifty stepfather planting its garden with the gay blossoms of the useful haricot-bean and the nasturtium. He had a frugal mind.

The petty tyrannies of the thrifty jeweller, his mean outlook on life, and his sordid aims, made of the habits and atmosphere of his class an even more uncongenial world for this brilliant girl to live in. Happily the pursuit of her art, and the friendship of that circle into which that art and her gifts and charming personality raised her, mitigated the tyranny of this sordid relationship. And, to add to her relief, Madame Suzanne, wife of the sculptor, and a friend of her mother, would carry off the girl with her into the country; and it was during one of their walks at Marly that she met for the first time Marie Antoinette.

On the 10th of May 1774, a month before Elizabeth Vigée's nineteenth birthday, King Louis the Fifteenth died of the small-pox — died without a friend, for he had dismissed the Du Barry in tears a short while before. His body was hastily thrust into a coffin, and hurried at the trot through the darkness to St. Denis, for fear of attack from the sullen crowds that gathered to do it dishonour; so was he huddled away amongst the bones of the ancient kings of his race, unattended by the Court, and amidst the curses of his people.

Louis the Sixteenth, son of Louis Fifteenth's only son, the dead Dauphin, ascended the throne of France in his twentieth year, a pure-minded, honourable young fellow, full of good intentions, and sincerely anxious for the well-being of his people; but of a diffident temper, timid, hesitating, and uncertain in decision, and under the influence of his young consort, the beautiful Queen Marie Antoinette, who had the imperious temper of her house, wedded to light and frivolous manners; she brought to her counsels a deplorable lack of judgment and a steadfast incompetence in knowledge of men.

The good qualities of this young pair had been very well in private life; but France needed greater abilities for her guidance than the simple virtues. It was a hideous part of the destiny of this young couple that they came to rule over a France that was passionately angered at the misdeeds of a king and his privileged class of nobles and clergy who had gone before them — of a class that had come unscathed through that reign, and were grown incapable of realising that they could not come unscathed through another.

The Du Barry flown, and her precious trio of ministers with her, Louis recalled the crafty old schemer Maurepas to power from the banishment into which the Pompadour had sent him; but he otherwise began well by making Turgot his minister of finance.

On the 25th of October in this 1774 that saw Louis Quinze and Marie Antoinette come to the throne of France, Elizabeth Vigée was elected to the Academy of St. Luke at nineteen years of age.

She brought to her early successes a charming modesty and an utter absence of conceit or of pose that added greatly to her reputation, and paved the way to further honours.

III

MARRIAGE AND MOTHERHOOD

But early success was not to be without black care stepping into the triumphal car in her procession towards an early and wide fame of this charming and accomplished young woman of twenty. Honours were easy. But the devil was in the machinery.

Her family had lived in the Rue de Cléry, opposite the hotel Lubert; thence they had drifted to the Rue St. Honoré hard by the Palais Royal; they now returned to the Rue de Cléry to the hotel Lubert itself. Here it chanced that Le Brun, the expert, carried on a lucrative traffic in pictures. His gallery attracted the pretty artist, who could study there at leisure the works of the great masters that passed through.

The two families soon became intimate. Le Brun carefully weighing the great advantages that such a union could bring to him, but entangled by his engagement to marry the daughter of a Dutch dealer in pictures who lived opposite to him, and with whom he had considerable business in works of art, beat about as to how he could marry Elizabeth Vigée. The girl was living in the splendour of a circle to which her family could not hope to aspire; the picture-dealer belonged to the middle-class in which her own family moved. Any day she might marry out of that middle-class world into the world of fashion. He saw that the girl moved in, and was happiest in, a great world to which he had not the key. He had the ambition to belong to that world, though his common-sense might have told him that he never could do more than hang about its outer courts. He was a calculating blackguard, a man of loose life, and a vulgar fellow with vulgar ambitions. He saw astutely enough that this girl was well on the high-road to considerable fortune. The Dutch girl opposite necessitated wary walking. He played the romantic lover, and before six months were run out he was pressing his suit, asking Elizabeth Vigée to marry him secretly.

PLATE IV. — PORTRAIT OF MADAME VIGÉE LE BRUN

(In the National Gallery, London)

She saw at Anvers the famous "Chapeau de paille" by Rubens. This canvas by Rubens clearly inspired her to the painting of the portrait of herself in a straw hat, where she stands bathed in the sunlight, her palette in her hand. The painting of the flesh of the pretty face is exquisite, and in spite of intense finish is broadly conceived and rich and glowing in colour. The clumsy drawing of the hand that holds the palette is the only defect in this, one of her masterpieces. The picture has the added interest of revealing to us how Vigée Le Brun set her palette. The thing is thrilling with life; and the little feminine conceit of wearing her black wrap is quaintly delightful.

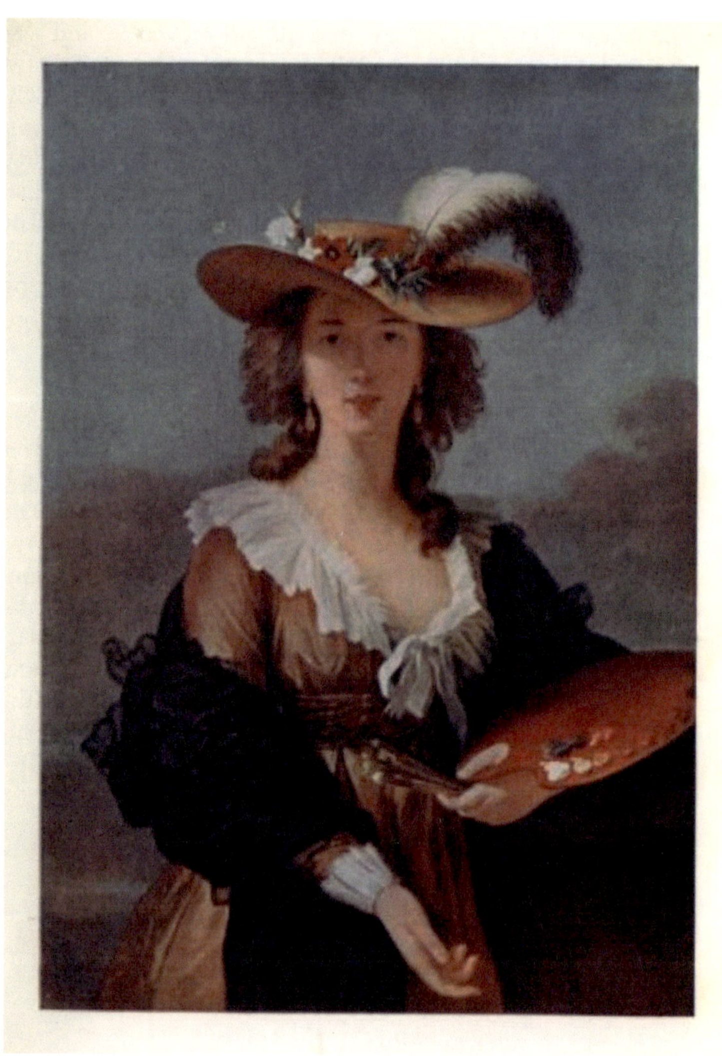

The girl seems to have had a presentiment of the misery that such a marriage would mean for her. After long and serious hesitation she gave her consent. It was perhaps due to a sense of being between the devil and the deep sea, for her sordid and miserly stepfather the jeweller must have been a sorry table-companion of her home life. If she suspected the picture-dealer to be a rogue, she thought, likely enough, that the more genial rogue would be a pleasanter fellow to live with than the other.

She married him secretly on the 11th of January 1776, on the edge of her twenty-first year. It was not a wholly promising beginning, this that gave her the name that she was to immortalise—Vigée Le Brun.

It was a sorry match. It began in secrecy; she was to discover that it was founded on a treachery. When the marriage was discovered it was too late to dissuade the girl from it; she had to listen to some plain home-truths as a Dutchman saw them, and to grim prophecies of the evil that would come of the business. But he might have spared his breath.

She was to have her ugly awakening. She early discovered that Le Brun was a gambler, a rake, and a thoroughly dissolute and un-scrupulous rogue. It was not long before he had not only squan-dered his own fortune, but was playing ducks and drakes with every penny that she gained by her art and her untiring industry.

She was soon to become a mother; the love that she had sedately allowed to go out to her disreputable and pretentious husband, and which she had early withdrawn in tatters, she now lavished upon this, her girl-child.

Meanwhile, her reputation increased by leaps and bounds. Her studio was simply besieged by "the Quality." The Duchess of Orle-ans had to wait her turn a whole year before she could be painted. Vigée Le Brun's praise was in every mouth. She was sung in prose and verse; the poetasters ran to much doggerel of handsome intent, as was the fashion of the day. Marquises and the rest of the scrib-bling folk tripped over halting feet to sing her charms and immor-talise her art. "L'orgueil de France" rhymed it to "la double puis-sance;" and "immortal crayon" to "admiration." They spilled the rosy inks. Le Brun, not the picture-dealing husband, but the poetical fellow who modestly nicknamed himself the Pindar of his age, plucked at the lyre with both hands in her honour.

Nay, have we not the written record that Laharpe, uttering his rhymed discourse on the genius of women to a great gathering of the bloods and wits at the Academy, and bursting into violent poesies in announcing that Elizabeth, "the modern Rosalba, but more brilliant than she, weds the voice of Favart with the smiles of a Venus"—every one rose to their feet, "not omitting the Duchess of Chartres and the King of Sweden," and turning to the blushing Elizabeth, applauded her "with transports"!

So much for France within the walls of the Royal Academy. But France without! The great minister, Turgot, baffled by the selfishness of the privileged classes, fell. But Louis called to power near as good a man, worthy banker Neckar. In an unfortunate hour for the Royal house, and against the will of the king, be it credited, and to the bewilderment of Neckar, the nation having gone mad with enthusiasm over the prospect of an alliance with Britain's revolted American colonies, war was declared against England, France undertaking not to conclude peace until the colonies were free. The success of the revolted colonies made the Revolution in France a certainty. The fall of Neckar and the setting up of the reckless and incompetent Calonne over the destinies of France brought the shout of the Democracy to the gardens of the king. Vigée Le Brun's picture of the dandified man certainly does not show him a leader of great enterprises. His reckless extravagance satisfied the nobles; it brought bankruptcy stalking to the doors of the king's palace. The distress and sufferings of the people became unbearable. The miserable scandal of the diamond necklace added to the discredit of the queen. The Royal family and the Court sank further in the people's respect.

As for Vigée Le Brun, she was come into her kingdom. And it is during those twenty years, from shortly after her marriage until she was forty, that her best and most brilliant portraiture belongs, before the hardness and dryness of her later style showed signs of the decay of her powers.

PLATE V.—THE TWO ELDER CHILDREN OF MARIE ANTOINETTE—THE FIRST DAUPHIN (born 1781, died 1789) AND THE MADAME ROYALE

(At Versailles)

The little Dauphin of four years, and his seven-year-old sister, the Madame Royale, seated on a bank, the boy's hat thrown at his feet upon the flower-strewn ground—a work in which Vigée Le Brun's colour-sense, her fine arrangement, and her feeling for style reach to their highest flight. The handsome boy was mercifully taken at the dawn of the Revolution; the girl was to know all its terrors.

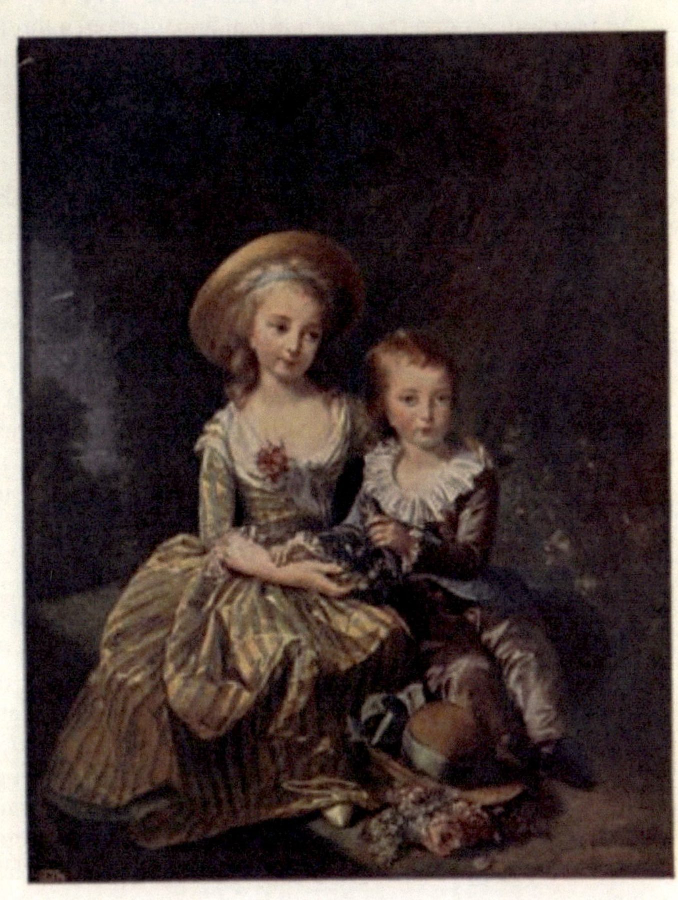

To its earliest, freshest years belongs the first portrait that Vigée
Le Brun painted, in her twenty-fourth year (1779) of Marie Antoinette, in which the young queen is seen with a large basket, and
dressed in a satin gown, holding a rose in her hand—painted the
year after the birth of her eldest child, the Madame Royale. Here is
no hint of the tragedy that was to overwhelm the handsome young
daughter of Austria; all was as yet but gaiety and roses and sunshine and pleasant airs and the glamour that hovers about a throne.
But there are signs of the imperious temper of her house, combined
with the levity and frivolity of manners, which were so early to
make her unpopular.

Vigée Le Brun was to paint her royal mistress close on thirty
times during the next ten years, until the prison doors shut upon the
Royal house of France; and there grew up between the two women
a subtle and charming friendship that was to make the talented
woman a dogged and convinced royalist to her dying day—indeed,
the temperament of women needs small incense towards the wor-
shipping of idols.

Vigée Le Brun was rarely more happy in her art than in several of
the many portraits she painted of herself about this time—more
particularly the two famous pictures of herself with her little daughter. "The Marie Antoinette with the Rose" is redolent still of the
eighteenth-century France—the siècle Louis Quinze. In Vigée Le
Brun's portrait of herself and her child we see in full career the
Greek ideals that were come upon France—a France weary of light
trifling with life, and of mere butterfly flitting from flower to flower;
here is that crying back to the antique spirit that was leavening the
middle-class of France which was about to claim dominion over the
land and to step to the foot of the throne and usurp the sceptre and
diadem of her ancient line of kings as the Third Estate; and to come
to power with violent upheaval, wading to the throne through
blood and terror. Here we see Vigée Le Brun, royalist, glorifying
motherhood, her arms and shoulders bare in chaste nudity, her
body scantily attired in the simple purity of Greek robes, her child
in her embrace.

Vigée Le Brun painted another portrait of herself and her little
girl-child; and she painted both, fortunately for her fame, when her

skill was at its increase. They stand out, with all their limitations, pure and exquisite as the Madonna and Child of Italy's finest achievement; for they were painted by a woman of genius with the passionate love of a child that is the wondrous heritage of woman; none the less religious in that it apes no show of religion. We see the age of free thought stating the innate religion of free thought; as Renaissance Italy painted paganism in religious disguise with the innate irreligion of its day.

In all her portraiture one is struck by the fact that Vigée Le Brun took much pains to arrange the draperies in what she considered picturesque fashion rather than that she painted the ordinary gowns of her day as her sitters wore them on entering her studio. And we have her own word for it in her *Souvenirs* (wherein the careful record of each picture that she painted may be found) that the dress of most women of the time seemed ugly to her—as it does to so many artists, generally not the best, in all times—indeed, she used every ounce of tact that she possessed in order to "arrange" the draperies. She sternly set her face against the use of powder and paint that the fashion of her century put upon complexions even of the most delicate beauties; and she always, when she could, arranged the hair of the women sitters. She tells, not without pride, how, having persuaded the beautiful Duchess of Grammont-Caderousse to put off paint and powder, and to allow her to arrange her jet-black hair, drawing it down over the forehead and separating it over the brow and arranging it in irregular little curls, the duchess went to the theatre as she was, and created the fashion thereby, in spite of the fact that Vigée Le Brun could never persuade the queen to give in to her, Marie Antoinette replying to all her beguilings: "I shall be the last to follow the fashion; I do not wish them to say that I am trying to hide my huge forehead."

Marie Antoinette was beginning to realise that all France did not fawn upon her with the courtier's bended shoulder or pretty speech.

IV

MARIE ANTOINETTE

In her twenty-seventh year (1782) Vigée Le Brun made a journey into Flanders with her husband, who had gone thither picture-dealing. The works of the Flemish masters that she there saw had a marked effect upon the increase of her art.

She saw at Anvers the famous "Chapeau de paille" by Rubens; and had revealed to her the beauties of a sun-flooded figure, with the face painted in the golden glow of reflected lights under the shadow flung down over it by a large hat. This canvas by Rubens clearly inspired her to the painting of the portrait of herself in a straw hat, where she stands bathed in the sunlight, her palette in her hand. The painting of the flesh of the pretty face is exquisite, and in spite of intense finish is broadly conceived and rich and glowing in colour. The clumsy drawing of the hand that holds the palette is the only defect in this, one of her masterpieces. The picture has the added interest of revealing to us how Vigée Le Brun set her palette. The thing is thrilling with life; and the little feminine conceit of wearing her black wrap is quaintly delightful.

Thenceforth her art has an added sense of style, a fuller statement of atmosphere; in her handling of paint and employment of colour she was soon to reach the very height of her achievement.

It was shortly after her return from this journey into Flanders that Joseph Vernet decided to put down her name for election to the Royal Academy. Her portrait of herself created such a sensation that her election became assured. She had to paint the usual formal *tableau de reception*, and chose Allegory, painting her "La Paix ramenant l'Abondance," which, though a somewhat stilted affair such as Academies demand, is full of charm—and is still to be seen at the Louvre. She was received into the Academy on the last day of May in 1783 in her twenty-eighth year, and thenceforward had the valuable privilege of the right to show at the Salon.

Vigée Le Brun had not reached to such rapid and wide success, in spite of all her charm and youth and the defence that chivalry should grant to her sex, without setting jealous tongues wagging. The "Peace bringing back Abundance" happened to be hung under a canvas by Ménageot, "The Birth of the Dauphin"; and comparisons between the two pictures were aimed at creating a slander which there were only too many ready to believe; for it was supported by certain facts which fell into place, and took on a suspicious air when pointed to as supporting evidence. This Ménageot, who afterwards became Director of the Academy at Rome, lived in the same house as Vigée Le Brun; and rumour soon got agog to the effect that he was in the habit of painting, or at any rate putting the finishing touches to, her work, Pierre, at this time first painter to the king, had employed this slander in order to oppose her election to the Academy; he was the leading spirit of a cabal against her, as soon became known; for he was the victim soon afterwards of a satirical jingle that went the round of the studios.

She was harassed also by the petty spites of enemies who did not hesitate to try and have her studio seized under the charge that she was painting without legal title since she had never been apprenticed to a painter. And malignant tongues whispered it abroad that she never would have been elected to the Academy had it not been done at the command of the Court. They made her very friendship with the queen a whip with which to lash at her. She was now painting many portraits of the queen.

Vigée Le Brun spent her entire day at her easel, from the time she arose in the morning, and she rose early, until the daylight went. She gave up dining in the town, in order not to be drawn away from her work; and the temptation must have been strong for a young and charming woman so greatly in request. But at nightfall she went out to social functions, and herself received the most brilliant and distinguished members of society and art and letters at her own house, giving concerts where Grétry, whose portrait she painted, and other celebrated musicians played portions of their operas before they were seen or heard upon the stage; whilst the grandees of the old noblesse and the famous wits frequented her house.

Again, the report of her receptions got noised abroad; and envious tongues were soon exaggerating the extravagance and luxury in which she lived, descending to such childish tittle-tattle as that she lit her fires with bank-notes, that the number of her guests was so great and so distinguished that, for lack of seats, the marshals of

France had to sit upon the floor; gossip and babble that were to cost her dearer than she thought, though she laughed it all away with a shrug of her pretty shoulders at the time. It was concerning one of her six-o'clock suppers that a slander was started which was to be a serious menace to her in after years.

PLATE VI. — PORTRAIT OF MADAME MOLÉ-RAYMOND

(In the Louvre)

This famous painting of Madame Molé-Raymond, the pretty actress of the Comédie Française, is one of Vigée Le Brun's masterpieces. Her brush is now at its most dexterous use; the laughing pretty woman is caught like a live thing and fixed upon the canvas as at a stroke as she trips across the vision, with muff upraised, smiling out upon us as she passes. Vigée Le Brun never stated character with more consummate skill than here; never set down action with more vivid brush, catching movement flying.

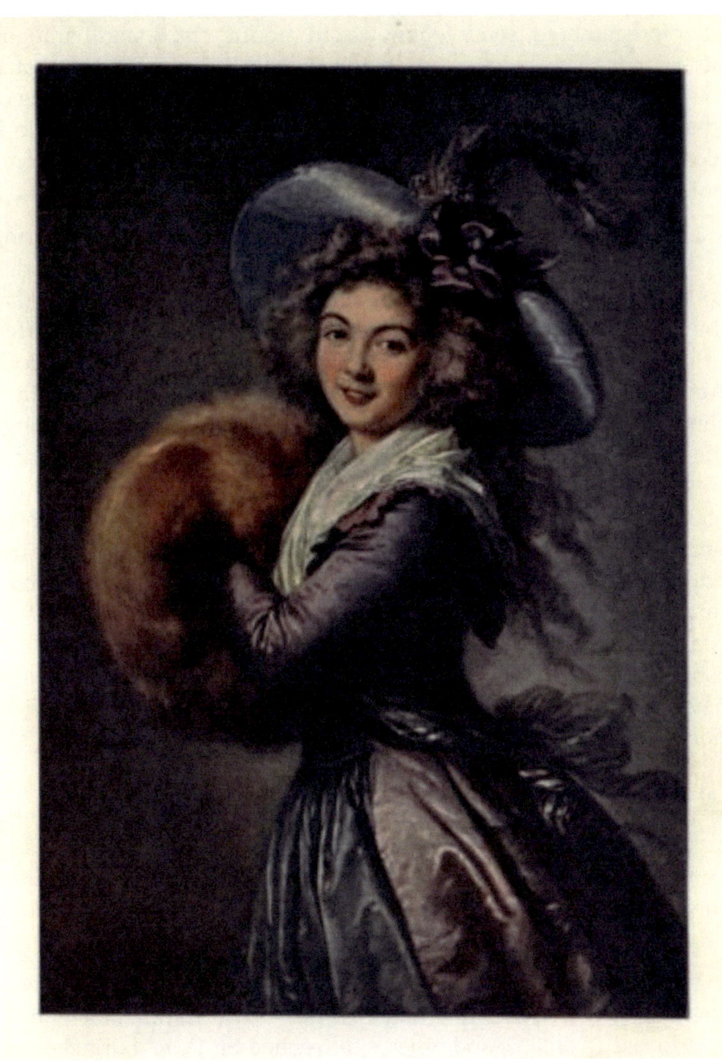

It was an age of small oratory. Every man who could string a neat sentence together, scribbled or harangued. It was boorish and an unfashionable thing not to be an author, a poetaster, a little orator, a critic, a dabbler in the arts. At coffee-houses or clubs, wheresoever men foregathered, some fellow would mount a table and harangue his friends. The bloods caught the vogue, little foreseeing that it made a hotbed for the airing of discontents, and for the parading of ideals which alone could blot out those discontents. All took to it like ducks to the village pond. There was much quackery; some honest noise.

Now it so chanced that at Vigée Le Brun's there was a gathering at which Le Brun—"Pindar" Le Brun the poet—spouting a discourse, described a Greek supper. The idea at once sprang up that they should have one straightway; they got up the cook and started to set the thing going, the poet guiding the making of the sauces. Amidst the general merriment Vigée Le Brun suggested that they should dress for the fantastic affair in Greek costume, and arrange the tables and seats after the antique fashion. So the jocular business went apace. It was a merry party of Athenians that sat down to the feast—"Pindar" Le Brun wearing laurels in his ridiculous hair, and a purple mantle round about him; the Marquis de Cubières tricked out with a guitar as a golden lyre; Vigée Le Brun being chief costumier to the frolic, draping Chaudet the sculptor and others in as near Greek fashion as could be. Vigée Le Brun, herself in white robes and tunic, and garlanded with flowers and veiled, seems to have presided over a rollicking gathering. The noise of the jollification got abroad.

The banquet cost the frugal Vigée Le Brun some fifteen francs in all; but in the mouths of the spiteful the tale of its extravagance quickly grew. A few days afterwards there was talk of it at Court; and the king was solemnly assured by "one who knew," that it had cost 20,000 francs.

This unfortunate Greek supper dogged her steps in the wanderings over the face of Europe that were to be her long exile. At Rome she was to discover that it had cost her 40,000 francs; at Vienna it was to rise to 60,000; and when she reached St. Petersburg she was to find that, gathering volume on the long journey, it had increased to 80,000 francs, when she scotched the lie and killed it; but not before it had served her a very ugly turn.

The truth was that she was being made to share the unpopularity that had fallen upon the queen. She was painting, and was on friendly terms with, not only the Royal Family, but with the unpopular ministers and servants of the crown, and with the noblesse, who in league with the queen were chiefly concerned in keeping the king from popular measures. She painted, according to the authorities, in 1785, in her thirtieth year, the portrait of Calonne though a parchment in the engraving from it bears the date 1787. The portrait of the minister set slander going against the artist, as regards the vast sum paid for it. The portrait of the seated minister ends below the knees; and it was of this picture of the weak Calonne, who clung so limpet-like to office, that Sophie Arnould, seeing it at the Salon, made the neat remark: "It is because he sticks to office that Madame Le Brun has cut off his legs." But whether she received much or little mattered not much to Vigée Le Brun; her husband seized and squandered all she earned. As a matter of fact, she received 3600 francs for the portrait from Calonne, sent in a handsome box worth 1200 francs—a couple of hundred pounds at the outside. It was a small price compared to the sums she was now receiving for portraits; Beaujou, the financier, paid 8000 francs (say 300 guineas); Prince Lubomirski 20,000 francs (£800)—not that the poor maker of these works gained thereby, for her precious picture-dealer husband had it according to his habit, and she had difficulty and a scene even to get two louis from the price when she asked the rogue for it. However, her reputation ever increased. She showed at this same Salon of 1785, in her thirtieth year, the portrait of the little Dauphin of four years and his seven-year-old sister, the Madame Royale, seated on a bank, the boy's hat thrown at his feet upon the flower-strewn ground—a work in which her colour-sense, her fine arrangement, and her feeling for style reach to their highest flight. It is perhaps the most wholly successful and most complete and masterly canvas of her long career. It hangs in Versailles, a pathetic comment, this happy moment in the children's life, when the days looked rosy and all the world was a beautiful garden.

At the Salon of 1787, in her thirty-second year, is record of a picture of "Marie Antoinette and her Children"; and of herself with her girl; and, amongst others, those of Mademoiselle Dugazon and of Madame Molé-Raymond. This famous painting of Madame Molé-Raymond, the pretty actress of the Comédie Française, is one of Vigée Le Brun's masterpieces. Her brush is now at its most dexterous use; the laughing pretty woman is caught like a live thing and fixed upon the canvas as at a stroke as she trips across the vision, with muff upraised, smiling out upon us as she passes. Vigée Le Brun never stated character with more consummate skill than here; never set down action with more vivid brush, catching movement flying; she never stated life more truly nor with more exquisite tact than in this bright vision of a dainty woman of the theatre.

Affairs in France were now in such a huddle that the State could not pay interest on the public loans. Calonne could no longer disguise the serious business from himself or the king. There was nothing for it but to call the Assembly of Notables. They met at Versailles on the 22nd of February 1787. Calonne fell, to give place to his enemy the turbulent and stupid Cardinal de Brienne. The Court was completely foul of the people when De Brienne threw up office in the midst of riots in Paris and throughout the country, and, in panic, fled to Italy, leaving the Government in dire confusion and distress.

The king took a wise course; he recalled Neckar. The convoking of the States-General now became a certainty. Paris rang with the hoarse cry for the Third Estate. The wrangle as to the constitution of the States-General became every day more dangerous.

The last portrait that Vigée Le Brun painted of the doomed queen was the canvas that hangs at Versailles known as "Marie Antoinette and her Children," in which the queen is seen seated beside a cradle with the baby Duke of Normandy on her knee, the little Madame Royale at her side, and the small Dauphin pointing into the cradle. When the doors of the Salon of 1788 were thrown open the painting was not quite finished; and for some days the frame reserved for it remained empty. It was on the eve of what was to become the Revolution, and the country was speaking now in no hushed whispers of the public deficit in the nation's treasury, and gazing bewildered at the bankruptcy that threatened the land. The empty frame drew forth the bitter jest: "Voilà le déficit!" The little Dauphin's pointing at the cradle was not to be without its significance—for the little fellow was to die at the outbreak of the Revolution and his place was to be taken by the babe on his mother's knee—the small Duke of Normandy was to become Dauphin in his place, and, in some few years, with his little sister, was to be made a close prisoner in the Temple. The king and the queen, separated from their children and each other, were to go out to the guillotine; the girl was to live through the seething hell of the Terror as by a miracle, and thereafter unhappily enough as the Duchess of Angoulême; but the fair boy, heir to one of the noblest heritages in all this vast world, torn from Marie Antoinette whilst the queen still lived, a prisoner, was to be handed to the tender mercies of the infamous Simon, jailor at the Temple, who was to train the frightened child to drink and swear and sing with piping treble the *camagnole*, until, hidden away in a tower of the prison, he was to die like a frightened hunted thing, his shirt not changed for months — die in darkness and squalor and in a filthy state. The guillotine did no mightier act of simple godlike vengeance than the day it sheared the skull from the foul neck of cordwainer Simon.

Marie Antoinette, in this the thirtieth portrait that Vigée Le Brun painted of her, is no longer the mere careless, gorgeous butterfly of some ten years ago when the little more than girl-artist first limned her features in the "Marie Antoinette with a Rose." The ten years that have passed are ending in solemn seriousness for the thirty-third birthday of the French Queen. The future is a threat. The people are demanding rule by Parliament — are singing for it — writing broadsheets claiming it.

It was about this time of stress and strain and anxiety at Court that, in 1788, Berger engraved so superbly one of Vigée Le Brun's greatest portraits, the consummately painted character-study, and exquisitely dainty colour-harmony of the Marchioness de Sabran.

The elections to the States-General took place amidst indescribable excitement throughout all France. The winter which went before the meeting of the States-General was terribly severe; it came on top of a bad harvest; the price of bread rose to famine pitch. Neckar generously sacrificed a vast part of his private fortune to buy food for the hunger-stricken poor of Paris. It was in national gloom that the States-General met at Versailles on the 5th of May in 1789. That day sounded the knell of the Monarchy.

PLATE VII.-MARIE ANTOINETTE AND HER CHILDREN

(At Versailles)

The last portrait that Vigée Le Brun painted of the doomed queen was the canvas that hangs at Versailles known as "Marie Antoinette and her Children," in which the queen is seen seated beside a cradle with the baby Duke of Normandy on her knee, the little Madame Royale at her side, and the small Dauphin pointing into the cradle. When the doors of the Salon of 1788 were thrown open the painting was not quite finished; and for some days the frame reserved for it remained empty. It was on the eve of what was to become the Revolution, and the country was speaking now in no hushed whispers of the public deficit in the nation's treasury, and gazing bewildered at the bankruptcy that threatened the land. The empty frame drew forth the bitter jest: "Voilà, le déficit!"

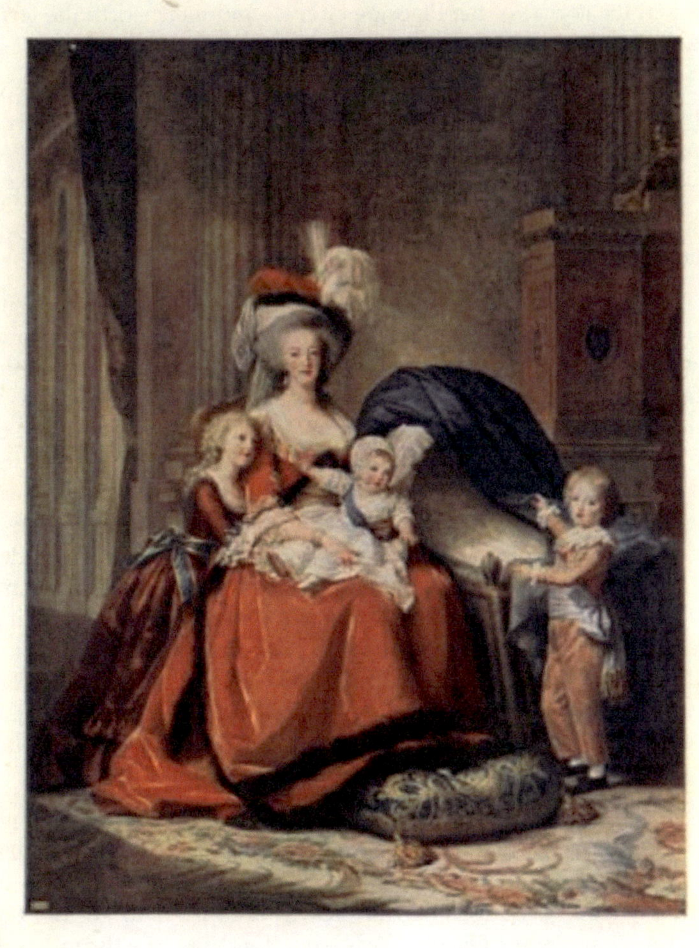

In little over a month the States-General was become the self-constituted National Assembly; a few days later, on the 20th of June, the deputies took the solemn oath in the tennis-court—the *jeu de paume.* At the queen's foolish urging the king fell back on force; filled Paris with troops under De Broglie; dismissed Neckar. The people at once took to arms. The 14th of July saw the fall of the hated Bastille. On the 22nd the people hanged Foulon to the streetlamp at the corner of the Place de Grève — and thenceforth the terrible shout *à la lanterne!* became the cry of fashion.

Such was the dawn of the Revolution in the streets of Paris, upon which Vigée Le Brun's eyes gazed down terrified in her thirty-fourth year.

Quickly followed the rumblings of the dark thunder-clouds that came up in threatening blackness behind the dawn — and which were about to burst with a roar upon reckless Paris.

The king showed astounding courage and considerable capacity during these awful days; but his work was constantly thwarted and ruined by the Court party and the queen. On the 3rd of October the officers of the regiment of Flanders were foolishly entertained at Versailles, and the whole Court being present, the white cockade of the Bourbons was distributed amidst rapturous approval, and the national tricolour trodden under foot. The starving rabble of Paris knew it, by the next day; and headed by a band of frantic women, set out for Versailles on the morning of the 5th of October, under the leadership of the ruffian Maillard who had distinguished himself at the capture of the Bastille. They overran the palace. The king again showed superb nerve; and the mob, abashed and admiring, calling "Long live the king!" withdrew to the courtyards. The unfortunate brawl in the courtyard followed; and the mishap of the night. The next day the Royal Family had to make their humiliating journey with the rabble to Paris.

Small hope for Vigée Le Brun, unless she stole out of France, and at once. She stood, indeed, in perilous plight. Her relations with the Court, and with the nobility, made every hour that she stayed in Paris a greater danger to her life. It was dangerous to go into the streets — dangerous to leave Paris — but for Vigée Le Brun more dangerous to stay. She was a marked woman. There was for her one sole way from death, and it was flight. By delaying she risked also the life of her child. Her friends begged her to be gone. She took the girl; searched hurriedly for all the money she could lay hands on — her husband had taken all but eighty francs (some three guineas) — and, leaving her canvases where they stood unfinished, she passed out of the studio that had been all the world to her; the place where she had spent the happiest hours of her life. A few days before, she had had to refuse to begin a portrait of the future Duchess de Noailles—to save her own head, not to paint those of others, was now become her single aim.

On the 5th of October of this year of 1789, that fearsome day that saw the rabble marching to Versailles, Vigée Le Brun took her seat in a diligence with her little girl, seated between a thief and a jacobin; the diligence rattled along the cobbles of her beloved city, and out of the gates—in such fashion Vigée Le Brun left Paris and took the road for Italy.

V

SWEET EXILE

As she rattled out of Paris between her grim companions, Vigée Le Brun little thought that her exile would last a dozen years; but everywhere she went she was destined to be welcomed with honour; and wheresoever she roamed—and she ranged across the face of the land wellnigh from end to end of it—she was to receive the same ovations, meet with the same success, be rewarded with the highest honours.

She went amongst strangers with but eighty francs in her purse out of all the fortune she had made by her dogged industry; she was to find in exile, not only a gracious home, but at last an immunity from the shameless squandering of her earnings by the disreputable thief whom she had married.

At Turin, her first halting-place, she tarried but a short while. She found that her name and fame had gone before her. At Bologna no French citizen was allowed to stay for more than twenty-four hours; but for Vigée Le Brun permission was brought without her asking for it. She spent three days gazing at the masterpieces of the Bologna School; and was made a member of its Academy.

At Florence she was asked to paint her portrait for the celebrated collection of portraits of famous artists by their own hand at the Uffizi Gallery.

At Rome the same impressive welcome awaited her.

Here she was soon at work again, with palette and brushes, upon the portrait of herself, which she had promised to the Gallery at Florence, where it now hangs—one of the most exquisite heads she ever painted, sunny, smiling, happy, with youth come back to it.

After eight months in Rome she moved on to Naples. Here it was that she painted the portrait of Lady Hamilton, Nelson's Emma, reclining by the sea, holding a cup in her hand as a Bacchante. Vigée Le Brun also painted her as a Sibyl—that picture which she took with her wherever she went, from town to town, and which always drew a crowd to her studio; whilst, grimly enough, Nelson's Emma rose to be one of the famed lovers of romance, to sink into want, and so to death in loneliness and misery at Calais.

It was at Naples, too, that Vigée Le Brun painted that portrait of Paisiello which she sent to Paris to the Salon, where it was hung as pendant to a portrait by David, and led to his high tribute to her genius, when, after gazing upon it for a long while, he said to his pupils: "They will think that my canvas was painted by a woman, and the portrait of Paisiello by a man."

Vigée Le Brun was now painting without cease. The Queen of Naples, her two elder daughters, and the Prince Royal, all sat to her.

During the first year of her exile the news from France had not been greatly alarming, and danger seemed to have been lulled. But at Naples she was to hear tidings that caused her bitter grief. First Neckar, finding himself out of touch with the king and the people and the Parliament, retired to Switzerland. Then, unfortunately for the king, Mirabeau died in the April of 1791. The king thenceforth resolved on escape. The Royal Family made their ill-starred flight to Varennes; to be brought back to Paris as prisoners. The constitutional party in the Legislative Assembly, at first dominant, soon became subordinate to the more violent Girondists, with their extreme wing of *Jacobins* under Robespierre and of *Cordeliers* under Danton, Marat, Camille Desmoulins, and Fabre d'Eglantine. The Proscription of all emigrants quickly followed—and the name of Vigée Le Brun was written upon the lists. The queen's enmity to Lafayette baulked, and completed the ruin of, the Royalist hopes. He retired into exile, and sadly left the Royal cause to its fate. On the 20th of April 1792 France entered upon her supreme struggle with Europe by declaring war. On the night of the 9th of August the dread tocsin sounded the note of doom to the Royal cause—herald to the bloodshed of the 10th of August. Three days afterwards the king and the Royal Family were prisoners in the Temple. There followed the terrible September massacres.

The National Convention met for the first time on the 21st of September 1792; decreed the first year of the Republic; abolished royalty and titles of courtesy; decreed *citoyen* and *citoyenne* in their place, and *tu* and *toi* for *vous*. It also proved the enmity of the two wings of the now all-powerful Girondist party—the Girondists proper as against the *Jacobins* or *Montagnards*. The conflict began with the fierce quarrel as to whether the king could be tried.

It was with sorrow at her heart that the exiled artist left Italy and journeyed into Austria. Having spent three years in Italy, roaming from town to town, and being received with honour wherever she went, she turned her footsteps to Vienna, where she remained from 1792 to 1795, her thirty-seventh to her fortieth years, again to be idolised, and painting hard the while. "To paint and to live are the same word to me," she was wont to say.

PLATE VIII.—PEACE BRINGING BACK PLENTY

(In the Louvre)

It was shortly after her return from this journey into Flanders that Joseph Vernet decided to put down her name for election to the Royal Academy. Her portrait of herself created such a sensation that her election became assured. She had to paint the usual formal *tableau de reception*, and chose Allegory, painting her "La Paix ramenant l'Abondance," which, though a somewhat stilted affair such as Academies demand, is full of charm—and is still to be seen at the Louvre.

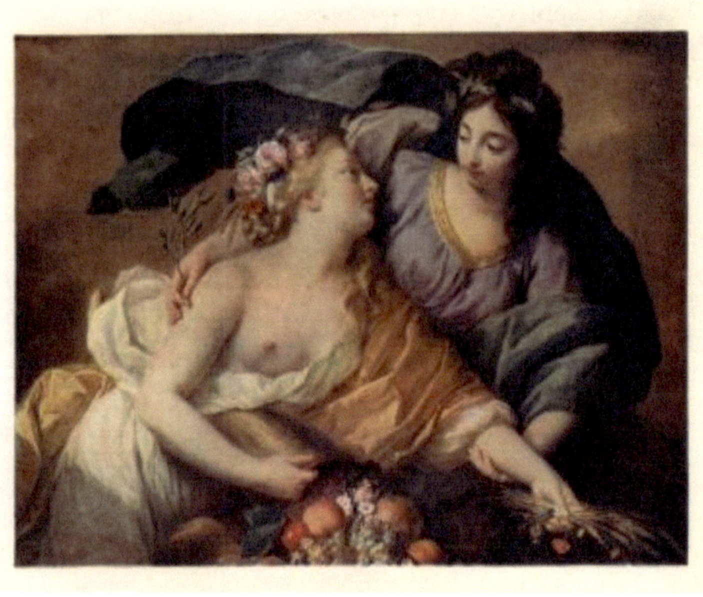

But these years in Vienna must have gnawed at Vigée Le Brun's heart like a fearful disease. In her France her much-loved Marie Antoinette was going through terrible days. The king was being tried for his life, and "Louis Capet" knew that he was a condemned man before he faced his accusers with the rare dignity and courage that keep his memory green. He was condemned to death,—Orleans, "Philip Egalité," voting with the majority amidst a murmur of universal horror even amongst the men who condemned the king. Louis' head fell to the guillotine on the 10th of January 1793. War with Europe followed; and the deadly struggle between the Girondists and Jacobins for supreme power. The 27th of May saw the appointment of the terrible Secret Committee of Public Safety. By June the Girondists had fallen. Charlotte Corday's stabbing Marat in his bath left the way clear to Robespierre's ambition. The Jacobins in power, the year of the Reign of Terror set in—from July 1793 to July 1794, with Robespierre as lord of the hellish turmoil. The famous "Loi des suspects" soon filled the prisons with some two hundred thousand miserable prisoners. The scaffold reeked with blood. During the year of the Terror the guillotine sheared the heads from fourteen hundred victims.

The unfortunate queen, Marie Antoinette, whose hair had gone white in a night, was tried as "the widow Capet," going to the guillotine with majestic serenity on the 16th of October 1793. The Girondist deputies followed; also the despicable Egalité Orleans, who went to his doom as the dandy he was, blotting out his many sins in a final dignity. Amongst the many batches came the miserable Du Barry, shrieking with terror, to her awful death, which she had brought upon herself by foolishly advertising a reward for a robbery from her house of Louveciennes.

Then came strife amongst the Jacobins themselves. Danton and Robespierre fought the bloodthirsty villain Hébert for life, and overthrew him; the Hébertists went to the guillotine like the curs they were. Danton, with his appeals for cessation of the Terror, alone now stood between Robespierre and supreme power; Danton, Camille Desmoulins, d'Eglantine, and their fellows went to the guillotine.

But other as able and resolute men had determined that Robespierre and his Terror must end; Robespierre went to the guillotine. The Revolution of the Ninth Thermidor put an end to the Terror in July 1794.

It was whilst at Vienna, in her thirty-ninth year, on the 3rd of June 1794, during the Terror, that Vigée Le Brun took out her act of divorce. And it was in this year that "citizen Le Brun" published in Paris his *Précis historique de la vie de la citoyenne Le Brun, peintre*!

In her fortieth year Vigée Le Brun went from Vienna to Prague; and, getting roaming again, passed through Dresden to Berlin and on to St. Petersburg, where she arrived in the July of this same year of 1795.

Her welcome in St. Petersburg must have been very sweet to the wandering exile. On the morrow of her arrival the Empress Catherine had her presented. She found at St. Petersburg many of her old friends, fled from the Revolution.

To her all Europe became a second country; but St. Petersburg her second home. Here, in fact, were larger numbers of those that had meant Paris to her than she could now have found in Paris itself. She was besides a spoiled child of the Court.

Her life at St. Petersburg was a very busy one. She settled down at once to the industrious practice of that art that was breath and life and holiday to her—working from morning until nightfall, and happy in it all. She painted something like forty-eight portraits in St. Petersburg. The Empress Catherine, now an old woman, was to have sat to her, and had appointed the day and hour, but her "to-day at eight" was not to be; apoplexy struck down her good-will; she was found dead in her room. The six years in St. Petersburg were amongst the happiest years of the artist's life, and the richest for her fortunes. Her reception into the Academy of St. Petersburg was almost a State triumph.

Meanwhile, the armies of France were winning the respect of the world by their gallantry and skill in war. The 23rd of September 1795 saw France ruled by the Directory. The 5th of October, the "Day of the Sections," led to Napoleon Bonaparte's employment as second in command of the army—the young general was soon commander-in-chief. And France thenceforth advanced, with all the genius of her race to that splendid and astounding recovery of her fortunes and to that greatness which became the wonder of the world.

The Revolution of the 18th and 19th of Brumaire (9th and 10th November 1799) ended the Directory and set the people's idol, Napoleon Bonaparte, at the helm of her mighty State as First Consul.

There was now little need—indeed there had not been for some time any need—for Vigée Le Brun to remain an exile; but, as a matter of fact, exile she had found to be so sweet a thing, so magnificent and perpetual a triumph, so delightful an existence, that Paris had early ceased to call her. Her experience with her rascally husband scarcely beckoned her back to her old home; she was now sole mistress of her considerable earnings. Besides, the Paris of her delight had been the Paris of Marie Antoinette—aristocratic Paris. Where was that Paris to be found? The personages and the atmosphere and the palaces and homes of all that Paris meant to her were gone into thin air—a sad memory. During her exile her mother had died; her last link with Paris died with her. She probably rarely gave the city of her youth's delight a thought, and likely enough never would have given it another serious one, had not destiny now struck her a blow which she bitterly resented; but which she should have foreseen to be as inevitable as death. Her daughter betrothed herself to, and married, a Russian, M. Nigris, secretary to the Count Czernicheff. Vigée Le Brun had been sorely tempted to oppose the match, for she foresaw that the girl would find no happiness in the union. She had poured out upon her child all the passionate love that had been so miserably thwarted in her own marriage. It had been more than bitterness to her to note that whilst her love for her girl increased, the girl's love for her seemed to dwindle. It was the bitterest blow that Vigée Le Brun had ever known; and she had been struck more than once. It turned the wanderer's eyes homewards to her wrecked Paris. Russia was no longer a delight to her. She became restless. The wander-fever came upon her; she got roaming; she went to Moscow for five or six months; but she could not settle—she decided to leave Russia.

The people amongst whom she had lived so long showed their affection, and personally appealed to her to make her home amongst them. The grandees went to her and told her of the sorrow that the news of her going had brought to them. The Emperor Alexander the First, himself, begged her not to leave them. She fenced all their kindnesses by promising to return soon. But during the forty years that remained to her she never set foot again in her "second home."

In her forty-sixth year Vigée Le Brun left Russia, and turned her face towards Paris; she crossed the border into Germany and halted a short while in Berlin to paint a few portraits, and in order to go to Potsdam to paint the Queen of Prussia. On leaving Berlin she narrowly escaped losing her diamonds and gold, a servant of the inn making an attempt to force open the baggage that contained them. From Berlin she roamed to Dresden, where she seems to have hesitated, reluctant to bend her steps towards Paris, yet torn with desire to go. As she came nearer to France her desire to return conflicted with her horror at the memories which the tragedy and wreckage of the Terror raised like ghouls in her imagination—every well-loved spot would now bear witness to her of the ghastly crimes that had swept away her old friends, their once masters and mistresses.

VI

THE END

At last, the year after Napoleon, with great pomp, took up his official residence as First Consul at the palace of the Tuileries, Vigée Le Brun set foot on French soil after twelve years splendid exile, carrying with her a considerable fortune.

The egregious Le Brun seems to have been reconciled, for he took a leading part in her reception. As she stepped out of the carriage she found herself in the arms of her brother and his wife, amidst tears of joy—with Le Brun in attendance. In her home, which was gay with flowers, everything else was exactly as she had left it, except that above her bed was a crown of golden stars set there by "citizen Le Brun." The long-suffering Vigée Le Brun was deeply touched; but could not forget that the unconscious wag had made her pay dearly for the golden stars.

Concerts and ovations greeted the returned exile; but it was all a strange world. A few old friends—and the rest, kindly strangers. She grew restless, and in six months was setting out for London. Here she found herself amongst hosts of old friends; and the doors of the great, as everywhere, thrown open to her. She painted George the Fourth and Byron amongst many others. The rage for portraits by her kept her in England for three years; and it was her fiftieth year (1805) before she returned by way of Holland and Belgium into France.

But in the midst of the great sea of adventure that swept France along under Napoleon she seems never to have got her bearings. She roamed to Switzerland twice, and painted some two hundred pastel landscapes of its scenery. It was during her first visit thereto that she met and painted Madame de Staël as "Corinne."

The years were increasing, the fever for travel cooled, and Vigée Le Brun, buying a house at Louveciennes, thenceforth passed her days between her country-house and town-mansion.

Death began to make gaps amongst such old friendships as the guillotine had spared to her. Le Brun died in 1813; her daughter in 1819; her brother the following year. Her art began to fail her. But her closing years were illumined by the affection and care of her two nieces, Madame de Rivière and Madame Trippier le Franc.

At five of the morning of the 30th of March in 1842, she died in her apartment at No. 29 Rue St. Lazare, in her eighty-seventh year; and was buried according to her wish at Louveciennes, where, in the church, still hangs the picture of "Ste. Genevieve" painted by her. Even her poor dead body could not sleep where she had willed; she was destined to gentle exile even after death. Her remains were moved to the new cemetery, and the simple tomb was again set up over them, whereon one may see a palette and brushes chiselled at its summit, and the grim words: "Here, at last, I rest."

PRINTED IN GREAT BRITAIN.

IN THE SAME SERIES

ARTIST. AUTHOR. VELAZQUEZ. S. L. BENSUSAN. REYNOLDS. S. L. BENSUSAN. TURNER. C. LEWIS HIND. ROMNEY. C. LEWIS HIND. GREUZE. ALYS EYRE MACKLIN. BOTTICELLI. HENRY B. BINNS. ROSSETTI. LUCIEN PISSARRO. BELLINI. GEORGE HAY. FRA ANGELICO. JAMES MASON. REMBRANDT. JOSEF ISRAELS. LEIGHTON. A. LYS BALDRY. RAPHAEL. PAUL G. KONODY. HOLMAN HUNT. MARY E. COLERIDGE. TITIAN. S. L. BENSUSAN. CARLO DOLCI. GEORGE HAY. LUINI. JAMES MASON. TINTORETTO. S. L. BENSUSAN. *Others in Preparation.*